I Saw Three ~~Ships~~ Skits Come Sailing In

A Trio of Modern Nativity Plays

by

Fay Rowland

Copyright

© Fay Rowland 2022

The right of Fay Rowland to be identified as the author of this work is asserted in accordance with the Copyright, Designs and Patents Act, 1988.

All rights reserved.

No part of this publication may be reproduced, stored in or introduced into a retrieval system, or transmitted in any form, or by any means (electronic, mechanical, photocopying, recording or otherwise) without the prior written permission of the author.

Visit the author's website at www.fayrowland.co.uk

Typeset by Attic Studios, England
in Century Gothic

Published by Thomas Salt Books

ISBN: 9781915150127

Using These Scripts

Permission is hereby granted to the owner to make up to 30 copies of each script for rehearsal and performance in educational and faith settings. You must not sell the copies and they must be destroyed after use.

If you do not own this book, you may not copy it.

If you make a recording of your performance, you may place the video on a non-commercial personal, church, or school website or video channel. You must include the following copyright notice at the end of your video.

Script by Fay Rowland
© copyright Fay Rowland 2022
All rights reserved. Used by permission
For further information visit www.reflectionary.org

If you wish to use this script for any commercial purpose, please contact the author (fay@fayrowland.co.uk).

Images © copyright by Revd Ally Barrett. Please visit *reverendally.org* for more artwork, hymns and poems, and for permission to use.

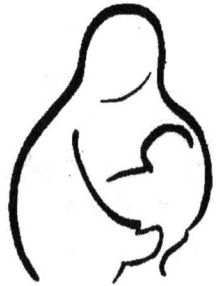

Amazon reviews for 'God Is With Us – Everywhere!'

 Phoebe

Totally recommend this easy to use, funny Nativity play

What an incredible gift this was for a Christmas during the coronavirus pandemic!

It is funny, easy to use and has quite a few small parts, which is great to get folks of all ages across the congregation involved. The parts were easily recorded separately and put together as a video.

We even managed to get the Moderator of the General Assembly of the Church of Scotland to play one of the wise men!

Fantastic resource and talented, helpful writer.

 Katie

Excellent Nativity Script

Performed this online via video recordings - everyone loved it. A great, meaningful script, beautifully written. Funny in places and very moving.

★★★★★ Mrs K L Holt

Brilliant

This is brilliant. What an amazing alternative and fun way of telling the wonderful story of Jesus' birth and reminding us of how God is with us in all things.

Acknowledgements

My grateful thanks, as always, to my children for putting up with a mum who is always going 'tappity, tappity, tap' on the keyboard and forcing them to eat pizza for tea. (Not sure that they mind, really.)

Thanks also to my venerable alpha-reader, Steve D, and to all those who have given constructive criticism on this and other projects.

Enormous thanks to Ally for her wonderful artwork. You'll find snippets of her work on the cover and scattered around, ensuring that the sections start on the correct-facing pages and beautifying what would otherwise be blank spaces.

Thank you, finally, to those who support my writing ministry at The Reflectionary. The resources there are given away for free because I believe this stuff is important, but I do still need to make a living! If you have not visited yet, may I encourage you to pop along to www.reflectionary.org?

By buying this book you are helping me to continue so, for being part of the team, gentle reader, THANK YOU! You're a star!

(That's always assuming you've actually bought this book. If you haven't, why not?)

Also Available as Single Titles

God Is With Us – Everywhere!
ISBN: 978-1-915150-03-5 (2020)

Christmas Gone Worng!
ISBN: 978-1-915150-08-0 (2022)

Away in a Suitcase
ISBN: 978-1-915150-10-3 (2022)

Contents

God Is With Us – Everywhere!

Casting, Costumes, Props etc	3
Script	13

Christmas Gone Worng!

Casting, Costumes, Props etc	37
Script	47

Away in a Suitcase

Casting, Costumes, Props etc	75
Script	87

God Is With Us – Everywhere!

A Rhyming Nativity Play

God Is With Us – Everywhere!

Tell the traditional story of God With Us, with some funny twists and a heart-felt message. Using rhyme to help performers deliver their lines, and with an adaptable cast size, this is the only play you will need this year.

The script is easy for children or adults to perform, while the nuanced message reminds us that Jesus is more than just a baby in a manger.

It's snappy and sassy, modern yet moving. We learn how everyone who met Jesus that first Christmas took home more than they brought.

Originally written as a Covid-safe Nativity, you can use this script for in-person or pre-recorded performances.

As they gazed in awe and wonder
at their baby, sleeping sound,
silently, beyond their vision,
all of heaven gathered round.

God no longer just in glory,
but right here where humans dwell.
God made flesh to be God With Us,
Jesus, our Emmanuel.

Cast

This script works for children, teens or adults, and can accommodate either a large or small cast. Whether you have a small Sunday school or you need to find parts for an entire classful of children, this drama can cope.

There are nine named characters plus a narrator, so the minimum is 10, but with the addition of non-speaking parts and splitting the narrator's lines, you could have thirty or more people taking part.

Character	Number of verses
Narrator	33 (you can split this role)
Gabriel	11
Mary	9
Joseph	7
Amos (shepherd)	3
Seth (shepherd)	3
Colin (apprentice shepherd)	3
Melchior (wise man)	3
Caspar (wise man)	3
Balthazar (wise man)	3

Casting

Although angels are often thought of as girls' roles, in the Bible, angels are male, and can be scary!

Gabriel in this play is not a cutesy little girl with blond pigtails. You might consider casting a tough-looking youth who can carry off the comedy section after he realises he has scared Mary. Gabriel has the largest speaking part apart from the Narrator(s).

The wise 'men' are scientists, so can be male or female.

Non-speaking parts

If you wish to include young children, you can add as many non-speaking parts as you like.

Children can dress up as donkeys, cows, or any other farm animal for scene 3, as angels or sheep for scene 4, or as camels or stars for scene 5.

For in-person performances, they can sit along the front of the stage and stand up during the appropriate scenes.

For virtual performances, each one can record a short video making an appropriate noise ('moo', 'baa', 'twinkle'). You can insert these between the spoken verses for maximum cute appeal.

Narrator(s)

The Narrator has 33 verses to speak in total, so you may wish to share this role among several people. There are different ways to do this, depending on how many people you want to include:

- A single Narrator can read all the verses
  1 narrator, total cast = 10

- You could have a small team (eg, 4) taking the verses in turns
  4 taking turns, total cast = 13

- You could have a different Narrator for each scene
  6 narrators, total cast = 15

- You could have small teams for each scene, taking the verses in turns
  2 taking turns for each scene, total cast = 21
  3 taking turns for each scene, total cast = 27

The reflective section at the end of scene 5 has the Narrator(s) speaking six consecutive verses. If you are performing in person, the wise men could sit down for this part, so that the focus is on the Narrator(s).

Narrators should be confident readers, but do not need to learn their lines. Their words can be printed out in large type and placed inside a Bible. The narrators then appear to be reading the Bible story (albeit slightly paraphrased!).

Costume Suggestions

You can use traditional or modern costumes, or a mixture of both.

Narrator(s) Christmas jumper and tinsel
Gabriel Halo and wings, plus jeans, shades and leather jacket, or traditional white robe
Mary Blue dress or hoodie, plus head drape
Joseph Construction worker or Joseph costume
Amos/Seth Farmer or shepherd costume, with beard
Colin Farmer or shepherd costume, no beard
Mel/Cas/Bal Scientist or wise man costume

Props

- Mary and Joseph have phones (scene 2)
- Joseph has a letter (scene 2)
- Mary has a wallet or credit card (scene 2)
- Mary has a cushion for a 'bump' (scene 2 & 3)
- Colin needs a sheep or some 'wool', eg cushion stuffing (scene 4)
- Balthazar needs a book or chart of stars (scene 5)
- All wise men need gifts (scene 5)

Everyone (including Narrators) needs a doll wrapped in a blanket for baby Jesus (scene 6). These should be kept hidden until noted in the script.

Staging

The script is divided into six scenes. You can spread them throughout a service, with songs and readings between, or you can run them back-to-back for a continuous story.

Staging – in person

There is no scenery needed, but you can use three chairs (preferably wooden) as minimal scene-setting if you wish.

Scene 1 – arrange the three chairs in a row as a sofa. Mary can sit in this when she feels faint.

Scene 2 – arrange two chairs as a work bench and Joseph can be working on the third. Later, when Mary needs to sit down, she can sit on the chair that Joseph has finished.

Scene 3 – arrange two chairs as a manger, with the third chair to the side for Mary to sit on.

Scene 4 – arrange the chairs in a curve around an imaginary fire for the shepherds.

Scene 5 – arrange the chairs in a row facing sideways. The wide men can sit in them as camels.

Scene 6 – arrange two chairs facing front and one chair behind. As each character says their lines, they join the tableau: Non-speaking characters enter at the start of the scene, kneeling across the front; then Mary and Joseph on the two chairs; all other speaking characters in an arc around; and finally Gabriel, standing on the chair at the back.

Staging – virtual

This play has been designed to work for worship where people cannot gather together. In this situation, the title is especially poignant: God Is With Us – Everywhere!

Each character should record their lines separately, starting a new video when a new person speaks. You can combine the clips one after another, trimming the ends, to make the final video.

Make sure that everyone films in landscape!

It looks good to have a photo of each person holding their Jesus doll and combine these into one image for the opening and closing titles.

For the final verse, you can make a video mosaic if you have that technology, or use the mosaic photo over everyone saying the last verse. If that is too tricky, have the narrator say those lines instead.

Hints and Tips

All the verses have the same rhythm as 'Tinker, Tailor, Soldier, Sailor':

DUM dee DUM dee DUM dee DUM dee
DUM dee DUM dee DUM dee DUM

This is to help people remember their lines and to keep a steady flow, but characters should not sound too 'clumpy' or mechanical when they speak.

It very, VERY much helps if characters can learn their lines, especially when filming videos, when they only have to learn the lines for one section at a time.

The words in square brackets and italics *[like this]* are stage directions. Don't read them out, do them!

Unless otherwise indicated, characters enter at the start of their scene and exit at the end.

God Is With Us – Everywhere!

The Script

Scene 1   At Mary's Home

Narr   Welcome to our Christmas story,
we re-tell it every year:
How God came from heaven's glory,
came to make his home right here.

Jesus, lying in a manger,
born in all our mess and fuss,
made us friends who once were strangers,
Son of God who lives with us.

Soon we'll meet the shepherds, wise men,
all the usual Christmas crew
and, perhaps, another story -
one that's now involving you.

In our world of joy and darkness,
in our laughter, pain and care,
Jesus came so we could know that
God Is With Us – Everywhere!
[Spreading arms wide]

So our story starts as always
with an angel, Gabriel,
visiting the home of Mary.
Was she busy? Who can tell?
[Shrugging shoulders]

Mary [Sweeping busily]
All today I'm cooking, sweeping,
feed the chickens, knead the dough.
[Miming jobs]
Honestly, it's never-ending!
Time to sit down for a mo.
[Sitting down, looking tired]

Narr But as soon as Mary rested
someone knocked upon her door.
[Knocking sound]
Grumpily she went to answer,
not expecting what she saw.

Gab [Looking impressive, with loud voice]
Greetings, Mary, highly favoured.
I have come to you from God
with a message straight from heaven.
[In a normal voice]
Oh! You look a little odd.

Yes, I realise you're frightened,
seems to happen quite a lot.
People see the wings and halo –
gives them all a nasty shock!

[Concerned and caring]
Would you like a glass of water?
Do sit down dear, there's a love.
That's much better. Here's the message
I have brought from God above.
[Clearing throat, ready to start again]

Narr Gabriel explained to Mary
God had chosen her to be
mother of a special baby –
God's gift for humanity!

Mary *[Looking confused]*
Ummn, don't want to seem ungrateful,
but there's just one tiny thing
I should mention, just in passing.
See my hand? No wedding ring!
*[Showing both sides of left hand,
like in the song 'Single Ladies']*

Gab Mary, don't get all Beyoncé!
It's OK, the child will be
not the son of your fiancé,
but of God, the one in three.
[Fingers showing 1 then 3]

Father God will send his Spirit
and become the Holy Son.
So the child you'll bear will be the
Son of God, the three in one.
[Fingers showing 3 then 1]

Mary Wow! That's quite a thing you're asking,
God himself will come to stay?
But I am the Lord God's servant.
Let it happen as you say.
[Bowing slightly, hands in prayer shape]

Narr So the angel bowed and left her.
Mary sat and drank some tea,
[Miming drinking tea]
called up her fiancé, Joseph.
What would his reaction be?
[Shrugging shoulders]

Scene 2   Joseph and the Angel

Narr   Right across the town from Mary
Joseph had a woodwork shop.
He was busy making benches
when a phone call made him stop.

Joseph   *[Answering phone]*
Joseph here, all tables mended,
doors and windows, fences too.
[Looking proud]
Carpenter to all of Naz'reth.
Who's there? Mary? Oh, it's you!

Mary   *[Talking on phone]*
Joseph dear, I've news to tell you:
we are going to have a child.
God's own son, an angel told me.
[Looking worried]
Now, please Joseph, don't get riled.

Joseph   *[Looking shocked and sad]*
Mary, this is disappointing.
Not that I am mad or cross,
but I must do what is righteous.
[Shaking head]
Sorry, but the wedding's off.
[Puts phone down and sighs]
*[**Mary** exits and adds cushion 'baby bump']*

Narr Joseph planned to do this quietly,
caring still for Mary's plight.
Gabriel had news for Joseph
In a dream, that very night.

Gabriel *[Enters, hands around mouth, calling]*
Joseph, son of David, listen!
You are frightened. That's OK.
[Thumbs up]
It's alright to marry Mary,
you'll still have your wedding day.

Mary said the babe she's bearing
is from God, and that is right.
Call him Jesus (which means saviour).
He will be this dark world's light.
[Exits]

Narr Joseph made it up with Mary
and they set a wedding day,
but before they picked the bridesmaids
something happened – Ah! Oy Vey!
['Oy Vey!' is a Jewish phrase like 'Oh no!']

Joseph *[Waving letter]*
Mary, I've just got this letter.
Not good news, cos it's from *Them*
(you know, Romans), 'bout our taxes.
Time to pay - in Bethlehem!

Mary *[Enters, looking shocked]*
What? You mean we've got to travel
while I'm pregnant? That's too hard.
Can't we pay by direct debit,
Visa Pay or Mastercard?
[Waving wallet or card]

Joseph *[Shrugging shoulders]*
Sorry sweetie, not invented.
It is Bethlehem or bust.
I'll start packing. Put your feet up.
Comfy footwear – that's a must.

Scene 3   By the Manger

Narr   So to Bethlehem they travelled,
('cos of Joseph's family tree)
walked for days and days to get there.
Were they tired? Guess we'll see.
[Shrugging shoulders]

Joseph   *[Walking on the spot]*
Nearly there now, Mary darling,
won't be long till supper time.
We can stay with Bob, my uncle,
in his guest room, you'll be fine.

Mary   *[Walking on the spot, leaning backwards]*
Really hope so, Joseph dearest.
Baby's nearly on his way.
When we get there, call the midwife.
Think you'll be a dad today!
[Patting tummy]

Narr   Uncle Bob had made it lovely
but the room was very small.
Mary much preferred it downstairs,
just beside the donkey's stall.

So that night, as stars were twinkling
Mary's tiny babe was born.
Joseph filled the donkey's trough with
hay and blankets, soft and warm.

Joseph *[Picking up baby Jesus doll]*
Can I hold him? Will he like me?
Do you think he'll call me 'Dad'?
[Eeew!]
God's own son just wet his nappy.
Mary, dear, you're looking sad.
[Noticing Mary]

Mary *[Looking at baby Jesus doll]*
I was thinking, will he be a
carpenter like you, you reckon?
Making chairs and tables, or does
something very diff'rent beckon?

[Wondering]
Will he grow to be like you, or
will he take his Father's job?
Nestling in your arms I see the
face of human, soul of God.

Narr As they gazed in awe and wonder
at their baby, sleeping sound,
[Looking around and above]
silently, beyond their vision,
all of heaven gathered 'round.

God no longer just in glory,
but right here where humans dwell.
[Opening arms wide to include everybody]
God made flesh to be *God With Us*,
Jesus, our Emmanuel.
[Bringing hands together to present baby]

Scene 4   Shepherds and Angels

Narr Meanwhile, on a distant hillside
shepherds sat there, tending sheep
Amos, Seth, apprentice Colin
round the campfire, half asleep.
[Yawning]

[Suddenly awake]
All at once, they heard some singing,
saw a brilliant shining light.
Gabriel arrived in glory.
[Looking scared]
What a terrifying sight!

Amos *[Looking up, scared]*
What the flippin' 'eck is 'happenin'?
Seth and Colin, wake up now!
Aliens, I think, or Martians!
Don't look at 'em! Hit the ground!
[Lying flat on face]

Gab *[Apologetic]*
Sorry, didn't mean to scare you
(it's the halo, I suppose),
but I have some information.
'Scuse me while I strike a pose.

[In 'hero' pose]
Do not fear, I bring glad tidings!
News of joy for all the earth.
News about a special baby.
News about a new king's birth.

Seth Get up off the ground there Amos!
There's no need to hide your face.
[Doing 'face-palm']
Martians? It's a bloomin' angel,
not some dude from outer space!

Colin [Pointing upwards, amazed]
Look, there's loads now, singing, "Glory,
glory be to God on high.
Peace on Earth to everybody."
Angels filling all the sky.

Gab [Pointing sideways]
Hurry now to David's city,
Bethlehem, and you will see
wrapped in cloth and in a manger,
Lord of all eternity.

[Slight pause, then not in rhythm:]
Get a move on then!
Don't just stand there gawping.

Narr So the shepherds left the hillside,
and, just off the city square,
found the house with Mary, Joseph
and the baby lying there.

Amos *[Beaming]*
Ain't he lovely? Who'd have thought it?
Me, old Amos, standing here,
right before the Lord of Glory!
Makes me knees come over queer.
[Wobbling knees]

Seth *[Scratching head]*
Feel I should have brought a present.
Could not think of what to bring.
What could shepherds give a baby
Lord of lords and King of kings?

Colin *[Showing wool (cushion stuffing) or sheep]*
I brought wool for him to sleep on,
comfier than straw and hay.
[Sniffing wool / sheep]
Smells of sheep I know, but this is
from the heart. Is that OK?
[Offering wool / sheep]

Narr So the shepherds knelt and worshipped,
[Looking down then looking up]
feet on Earth and eyes on heaven.
Jesus slept and snuggled softly
on the wool that they had given.

Sure, it had no fancy wrapping.
[Shaking head]
Ribbons? None, nor sparkly bow.
But the gift they gave to Jesus
[Nodding]
came with love instead of show.

So, as Colin, Seth and Amos
went back to their dozing sheep,
Jesus somehow went there with them,
giving <u>presence</u> they could keep.

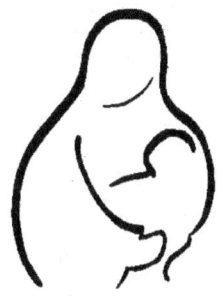

Scene 5   Wise Men Visit

Narr   Later on, a group of wise men
travelled in from lands afar.
Scientists, we'd call them these days,
following a bright new star.
[Pointing and looking upwards to star]

Mel   *[Riding on camel – pretend, obviously]*
Are we nearly there yet, Caspar?
We've been travelling for weeks.
Can you just remind me why we've
come, and what it is we seek?

Cas   Melchior, have you forgotten?
Honestly, you noodle-brain!
[Showing gift]
We bring gifts to greet and welcome,
celebrate a new king's reign.

Bal   *[Pointing to book or chart]*
All our books and all our wisdom,
told us that this star so bright
means that king and God and saviour
will be born this very night.

Narr When the wise men stopped their journey
what they found was quite a shock:
Mary, Joseph, babe in manger,
shepherds outside with their flock.

Mel Can I check, this *is* the right place?
I brought gold to crown a king,
[Presenting gift]
but I wonder, where's the palace?
Is this manger quite the thing?

Cas I brought incense, pure and holy,
made to worship God on high.
[Presenting gift]
Is this baby, weak and helpless
Mighty God with human cry?

Bal I brought myrrh, which symbolises
one who dies to save us all.
[Presenting gift]
Seems a strange gift for a baby,
job too big for one so small.

Narr So the wise men gave their presents
though they did not understand
how the child who lay before them
would, one day, give this command:

"Follow me!" he'd call to many,
preach Good News in all he said,
heal the sick and free the captives.
Would they follow where he led?

Gave his life to pay our ransom,
bought us all at costly price.
Righteous king and God and saviour.
Perfect lamb as sacrifice.

Raised to life to raise us with him,
Victor, Christ and Living Word.
All this lay before the baby
sleeping soundly, undisturbed.

So the wise men knelt around him,
gave their costly presents, then
suddenly, they knew that they'd be
taking treasure home with them.

Richer than the purest incense,
costlier than gold or myrrh,
wise men took home truest Wisdom,
Prince of Peace and Comforter.

†

Scene 6   God Is With Us

Narr   Now our story's almost ended.
Everyone has met him here.
Will you take the Christmas baby
home with you throughout the year?

Let us hear from all the people
who have met with God today.
How will this affect their stories?
Will this change them? Who can say?
[Shrugging shoulders]

Mary   Strangest night, but stranger morning.
Joy and sadness like a sword.
When I kiss my baby's forehead
I believe I kiss my Lord.
[Holds up Jesus doll, then joins tableau]

Joseph   Though I'm his adopted father
I will raise him as my son,
teach him all I know and love him,
serve my King 'til kingdom come.
[Holds up Jesus doll, then joins tableau]

Amos   I don't really understand it,
all the stuff the angels said,
but I know I knelt and worshipped
by the Lord Almighty's bed.
[Holds up Jesus doll, then joins tableau]

Seth Why would God come down to shepherds,
poorest folk of all the poor?
Live with us and make us worthy
I don't know, but I adore.
[Holds up Jesus doll, then joins tableau]

Colin What have I to give to Jesus?
Nothing, but yet everything.
All my heart and soul and worship,
for the baby, God and king.
[Holds up Jesus doll, then joins tableau]

Mel Gold I brought, expecting royals,
Majesty I found instead.
Higher King than all kings ever,
lying in a manger bed.
[Holds up Jesus doll, then joins tableau]

Cas I brought incense, made for worship,
rising as a prayer to heaven.
Prayers now answered by the baby,
God's own gift to me is given.
[Holds up Jesus doll, then joins tableau]

Bal Myrrh I brought, not understanding
how this babe would die and live,
bringing life in all its fullness –
gifts that only he could give.
[Holds up Jesus doll, then joins tableau]

Gab So God's plan before creation,
Earth in heaven and heaven on Earth,
came in form of gentle baby,
Mighty God in human birth.
[Holds up Jesus doll, then joins tableau]

Narr Now Emmanuel is with us,
Christmas is forever true.
In your home, if you'll invite him,
God with you and you and you.
[Holds up Jesus doll]

God on Earth and God in heaven,
God with every human heart.
Greatest gift of all gifts given:
We and God no more apart.

All Shout with us the Christmas story.
Let all heaven and Earth declare:
Jesus came to Earth from glory,
[All shout together]
God Is With Us – Everywhere!

Christmas Gone Worng!

An All-Age Nativity Play

Christmas Gone Worng!

Welcome to this light-hearted Nativity play telling the traditional Christmas story with the help of carols, but where everything goes a bit *worng*. There is a stroppy Mary, a confused wise man and an angel who ... well, you'll have to read the script to find out.

The script incorporates readings from the gospels of Matthew, Luke and John in an easy-to-read translation.

The theme of the play is that God came to us at Christmas, despite things not being perfect. Immanuel, God With Us, even in our mess and muddle.

It is suitable for a school production such as a Nativity play or Christmas assembly, or at church as part of All-Age Worship, Messy Church, Crib Service or a Carol Concert.

Running time is approximately 22 minutes including readings, carol excerpts and talk, but excluding any songs or carols you may wish to add between scenes.

Cast

The script can be performed by a minimum of two payers, up to a cast of thirty or more. You can have adults, children or even puppets playing the roles.

Speaking Parts

- **MC** — Master of Ceremonies
- **Reader** — Reads Bible passage
- **Soloist** — Sings unaccompanied (could be recording)
- **Mary** — Stroppy teen
- **Joseph** — Irritated carpenter
- **Amos** — Shepherd's union rep
- **Bal** — Balthazar, wise man
- **Harold** — Angel, bit of a twit

Other players can be part of a choir (which does more than just sing) or non-speaking stable animals, stars, angels etc.

The script incorporates a seasonal message. This can be read by MC, or you could have a minister or head teacher step in at that point. You can replace the message with you own talk if you want.

Casting with Various Numbers

You can adapt the cast to suit your players, from 2 to 60.

If you have a limited number of people, one person can play several roles. There is time between the scenes for a single actor to change costume for the five named characters, although this will mean they cannot form a tableau on stage.

If you need to accommodate a large number of actors, the roles of shepherd and wise man can be split between three, either three speaking roles or one speaking and two non-speaking as preferred. You can also share the Bible readings between several readers. There is a reading for each of the five scenes, so this can accommodate five, ten or fifteen readers.

Younger children can have non-speaking roles as sheep accompanying the shepherds, and other stable animals, angels, stars etc, joining the tableau at the end for a truly Instagram-worthy scene.

In addition, the choir plays a vital role, more than simply leading congregational songs (if used). There really is a place for everyone!

Example casts

Cast of 2
- MC + all readings
- All other characters
- Soloist and choir are recordings, cast or live

Cast of 6
- MC + all readings
- Mary
- Joseph
- Amos
- Balthazar
- Harold
- Soloist and choir are recordings, cast or live

Cast of 10
- MC
- Reader
- Mary
- Joseph
- Amos
- Balthazar x 3
- Harold
- Soloist
- Choir is recordings, cast or live

Cast of 30+
(16/21/26 speaking + choir + non-speaking roles)
- MC
- Reader x 5 (or 10 or 15)
- Mary
- Joseph
- Amos x 3
- Balthazar x 3
- Harold
- Soloist
- Choir
- Non-speaking stable animals / angels / stars

Tableau

If you use different actors for the main characters, you can assemble a tableau on the stage, with each character joining it after their scene.

You will need a chair in the centre with enough space in front for the action, and a stool behind the chair.

Mary sits centre-stage after scene 1. Joseph stands beside her after scene 2. Amos and sheep kneel to one side after scene 3, and Balthazar to the other after scene 4. Harold stands on the stool at the end of scene 5.

Mary should surreptitiously produce baby Jesus, either from under / behind her chair or hidden in her clothes, ready for the final reveal in scene 5.

Small children sit with their appropriate characters to the sides and front so that they can be seen.

All tableau characters should lower their heads while other scenes are taking place so as not to distract the audience.

Non-speaking characters can enter at the same time as their speaking-part character, or at the start of Scene 5 together with children from the congregation dressed as characters. (Yes, even if that means three Marys and five wise men.)

You might like to have spare shawls, head drapes (tea towels and rope ties) and tinsel crowns to give to children who don't have costumes.

Costume Suggestions and Props

MC Master of Ceremonies.
Costume = modern dress.

Soloist Preferably an angelic child, looking like a John Lewis advert.
Costume = traditional robes or Christmas jumper.

Mary Costume = hoodie and jeans, blue shawl over head, plus hidden baby for tableau.

Reader Costume = modern dress.

Joseph Costume = high-vis and hard hat with 'tea towel' headdress, plus hammer or saw.

Amos Shepherd.
Costume = overalls and 'tea towel' headdress, plus staff / toy sheep.

Bal Balthazar, wise man.
Costume = posh suit with bow tie, turban / fez, plus gift.

Harold Angel. Preferably an old man.
Costume = all white, with tinsel, halo and wings, plus tutu if at all possible.

Hints and Tips

The words in square brackets and italics *[like this]* are stage directions. Don't read them out, do them!

Mary and Joseph should enter through the audience if possible, disturbing the soloist and choir. Amos and Balthazar can enter from opposite sides.

Balthazar needs to speak 'off stage' so will either need a microphone in the wings or speak from a place where he can be heard.

For the tableau, place a chair centre stage for Mary, with a stool behind for Harold. You can hide a baby doll under or behind the chair.

If you have lighting available, dim the lights at the back as the tableau assembles, keeping the front lights high to draw attention to the actors for each scene. Raise the back lights as the tableau is revealed in scene 5.

To give younger children a larger part than simply joining the tableau at the start of scene 5, add a couple of rounds of 'Little Donkey' while they parade around the hall before taking their places on stage.

MC can have their words on a clip board or on a lectern, if needed.

Christmas Gone Worng!

The Script

Christmas Gone Worng

Scene 1 – Mary

MC *[In 'Christmas advert' voice]*

Christmas, the most perfect time of year. A time of peace, joy and understanding throughout the world.

A time when families never argue, when gravy is never lumpy, and when Monopoly ends harmoniously with everyone winning, even Uncle Albert.

May I welcome you to our Nativity. We start in the traditional manner, with a reading and a carol telling the timeless story of our saviour's birth.

Reading from Luke 1:26-38

God sent the angel Gabriel to Nazareth in Galilee, to a young woman there. Her name was Mary. She was engaged to Joseph who was of David's family line.

The angel went into the house and said to her, 'Greetings Mary. God is pleased with you and is with you!'

What the angel said troubled Mary. She wondered what this greeting meant.

The angel said to her, 'Do not be afraid, Mary. God has blessed you. You will have a baby son. Name him Jesus. He will be great and will be called the Son of the Highest One. The Lord God will make him king where his father David was king. He will be king for ever.'

Then Mary said to the angel, 'How can this happen? I have no husband.'

The angel answered, 'The Holy Spirit will come to you. The power of the Highest One will be over you. So the holy child born to you will be called the Son of God.

Mary said, 'I am the Lord's servant. Let it be as you have said.' Then the angel left her.

Soloist *[Formal and traditional]*

🎜 Once in royal David's city,
Stood a lowly cattle shed,
Where a mother laid her baby,
In a manger for His bed:

*[**Mary** enters from back, walking up aisle and making a fuss while singer continues]*

🎜 Mary was that mother mild,
Jesus Christ, her little child.

Mary	Hold on! Hold on, just one tinsel-picking minute! What's all this about?
MC	What's all what about?
Mary	[Indicating singer] This! [Indicating Christmas decorations] This! [Indicating congregation] THIS!
MC	Ummn, we're celebrating Christmas. You know, when you had the special baby?
Mary	When I had the WHAT?
MC	God's son? Jesus? Ringing any bells?
Mary	[Getting cross] Huh? What are you on about? I ain't having no baby. Joseph and me have only just got engaged. We haven't even set the wedding day yet. Don't you go talking about some baby. You'll get people gossiping, and my Mum will never let me hear the end of it. [Muttering to self – what a load of old cobblers, having a baby, talking rubbish, I'd get it in the neck for sure, etc]
MC	Can I check, you are Mary, aren't you? From the carol. You know, [Singing] 🎵 'Mary was the mother mild ...'
Mary	[Hands on hips] Do I LOOK mild?

MC [*Backing off*] Ummn, No?

Mary And what's this about a cattle shed?

I'm sorry, but when I have a baby, I'm planning on midwives and a nice clean cot with fluffy blankets. And I ain't planning to give the baby a cow pat for a pillow!

MC [*Cautiously*] Do you mind if I say something?

Mary What?

MC Well, it's just that you seem a bit more ... stroppy that most Marys.

Mary I'm a teenager, what do you expect? And if there's going to be pregnancy hormones on top of that, well, all I can say is there had better be a LOT of chocolate!

MC Fair enough. I'll order a bulk pack.

Mary You do that.

[**Mary** *exits if playing all characters, otherwise sits on stage to form start of tableau*]

Suggested songs

Silent Night
Mary, Did You Know?
Mary's Boy Child

Scene 2 – Joseph

Reading from Luke 2:1-7

> About that time, the Roman ruler Augustus made a law that everyone must have their names written in a register.
>
> Joseph left Nazareth, a town in Galilee, and went to Bethlehem in Judea. This was known as the town of David. Joseph went there because he was from the family of David. Joseph went to register with Mary because she was engaged to marry him and she was going to have a baby soon.
>
> While they were in Bethlehem, the time came for her baby to be born. This was her first child, a son. There were no guest rooms, so she wrapped him in cloths and laid him in an animal's food box.

Choir [Keeping an eye out for trouble]

> Away in a manger
> No crib for a bed
> The little Lord Jesus
> Laid down his sweet head

[**Joseph** enters, making a fuss while choir sings]

> The stars in the bright sky
> Looked down where he lay

[Choir fades off and stops when Joseph interrupts]

🎼　　　The little Lord Jesus
　　　　Asleep on the hay

Joseph　Oh no, no, no. We're not having any of that. Very bad for my social media presence, that is. Can't be doing with this kind of bad press. I'm on Check-a-Trader, I'll have you know!

MC　I'm sorry, you are ...?

Joseph　*[Pause, giving MC a 'what planet are you on?' look]*
I'm Joseph. Who were you expecting, King flippin' Herod?

MC　No, no, of course you're Joseph. What's the problem, Joe? May I call you Joe?

Joseph　What's the problem? What's the problem, you ask? I'll tell you what the problem is.
I've got a business to run. Got a wife and kid to support.
And this kind of thing *[Indicating choir]* is bad for business. THAT'S what the problem is.

[Choir look offended]

MC　You don't like the choir? But I thought they were rather good.

Joseph　Not the choir. It's what they're singing. Makes me look bad.

MC　What do you mean?

Joseph Well, look at the words. 'Away in a manger ...'

MC *[Shrugs]*

Joseph '... No crib for a bed.'

MC *[Shrugs]*

Joseph Well do you think I hadn't made one? Do you think I planned for my kid to spend his first night in some wonky old food box from the back of the stable?

It didn't even have proper dovetail joints. Splinters everywhere, and had they oiled it and carved a little teddy into the headboard like I had done? Oh no. Just a box. That's what my son got.

And one of the legs was longer that the others so it wobbled like Gran after a couple of sherries.

MC *[Helpfully]* I suppose that helped rock the baby to sleep.

Joseph *[Glares]*

MC But no, no, I see how that must be very frustrating. You wanted to provide for your son, but you weren't able to.

Joseph *[Deflated]* No, nor my wife. I mean, what kind of a husband carts his wife halfway across the country when she's about to pop, eh? And then when we got there, I couldn't even get a proper room for her to have the baby in.

	That wasn't how I meant it to be. I'm such a failure. I bet God wishes he'd picked a different step-dad for his kid.
MC	Now, I'm sure that's not true, Joe. Didn't God send an angel to tell you to marry Mary?
Joseph	*[Still looking glum]* Yes, I suppose he did.
MC	So there you go. You'll be fine as a dad, I'm sure. And anyway, you're not the only one who messes up in this story. You should see some of the gaffs that other people make!
Joseph	*[Agreeing]* Yeah, tell me about it!
	[Pause]
	No, I mean actually tell me about it. Do the Bible bit.
MC	Oh right, yes.

*[**Joseph** exits if playing all characters, otherwise joins tableau]*

Suggested songs

Infant Holy, Infant Lowly
Calypso Carol (See Him Lying on a Bed of Straw)
Like a Candle Flame (God is With Us, Alleluia)

Scene 3 – Amos

[If using 3 shepherds, split parts as indicated]

Reading from Luke 2:8-16

> In the same part of the country, shepherds were in the field watching their sheep at night. An angel of the Lord came to them and a bright light from the Lord shone all around them. They were very much afraid.
>
> The angel said to them, 'Fear not! Listen, I bring you good news! This news will make you very glad. It is for all people. A saviour has been born for you today in David's town. He is Christ the Lord. This is the way you will know him. You will find a baby wrapped in a cloth, lying in a food box.'
>
> All at once a great number of angels from heaven were with the angel. They praised God and said, 'Praise God in the highest heaven! Peace on earth and loving mercy towards all people!'
>
> The angels left them and went back to heaven. The shepherds said to one another, 'Let us go to Bethlehem and see what has happened. It is the Lord who has told us about it.' They went quickly. They found Mary and Joseph, and the baby lying in the food box.

Choir [*With Amos in choir being silly*]

🎼 While shepherds washed their socks by night,
And hung them on the line,
The angel of the Lord came down,
And said, 'Those socks are mine!'

[***Choir** dissolves into confusion*]

[***Amos** enters from choir*]

Amos1 Heh, heh, heh! Finally got someone to sing the proper words.

MC What [*Indicating choir*] was that? What did you do the choir?

[***Choir** look dazed, fanning each other*]

Amos2 Oh, just changed a few words here and there. Much more fun, don't you think?

MC I suppose, but the choir seems a little traumatised.

Amos3 They'll get over it. Anyway, I can't stand the normal words.

MC What's wrong with the normal words? I think they're lovely.

Amos1 You wouldn't think they were so lovely if you'd been seated on the ground all night with rheumatism like mine.

Cold, damp grass – it's no good for the joints, you know. Give me a nice, comfy armchair any day. And a big slice of pizza.

MC [Stage whisper to Amos] I don't think you had pizza back then.

Amos2 [Waving away the objection] Details. Details.

Amos, by the way. Amos bar Laban.
[Offering hand] Union rep for the AA.

MC Alcoholics Anonymous?

Amos3 Noooo, you twonk! It's our union, Amalgamated Agriculturals, incorporating:

Amos1 BURP, the Bethlehem Union of Reapers and Planters;

Amos2 SPIT, the Society of Ploughing Industry and Technology;

Amos3 and SNOT, the Shepherding, (brackets, Night-time) Operations Team.

Amos1 Anyway, the union will be balloting members about possible strike action next week.

MC What? Why?

Amos2 We'd rather it didn't come to that, of course, but we have to look after the workers, especially in the light (no pun intended) of a recent incident.

MC [Looking confused] What are you talking about? What about the workers?

Amos3 For the compensation, of course.

Displaced sheep, loss of working hours, trauma and mental anguish caused by sudden fright, and don't get me started on the health and safety!

MC Oh, I see. Yes, it does sound like there are issues that need addressing. What can we do to help?

Amos1 I'm glad you asked.

Here's the list of requirements to bring our working conditions into line with government regulations:

[Consults list, either real or pretend, hands list to other Amoses if using a split role]

1 – that appropriate seating be provided for shepherds including orthopaedic chairs for those with back problems.

Amos2 2 – that in periods of inclement weather, shepherds be permitted to watch their flocks in centrally-heated observation huts via remote CCTV.

Amos3 3 – that the Angel of the Lord be reminded that, before the commencement of shining all around, he should ascertain that all those in the vicinity have been issued with, and donned, protective eyewear capable of filtering out the harmful effects of UV-A, UV-B and glory.

MC	That all seems perfectly reasonable to me. Is that everything?
Amos1	And we'd quite like an automatic sock-washer.
Amos2	But only if there's room in the budget.
MC	I'll see what I can do. Can I get back to the story now?
Amos3	Be my guest.

[**Amos** *exits if playing all characters, otherwise joins tableau*]

Suggested songs

Angels from the Realms of Glory
The First Nowell
O Holy Night

Scene 4 – Balthazar

[If using 3 wise men, split parts as indicated]

Reading from Matthew 2:1-11

> After Jesus was born, wise men from the east came to Jerusalem. They asked, "Where is the baby who was born to be king of the Jews? We saw his star as it rose and have come to worship him."
>
> The star went before them until it stopped above the place where the child was. When the wise men saw the star, they were filled with joy. They went to the house and saw the child with his mother, Mary.
>
> The wise men bowed down and worshipped the child. They opened the gifts they brought for him and give him treasures of gold, frankincense, and myrrh.

Bal1 *[Offstage]* Hang on a minute, I'm having trouble with my ... ooh ...

Bal2 *[Offstage]* That's a bit snug ... I just need to ... urggh, that's better.

Bal3 *[Offstage]* Anyone seen my shoes?

Bal1 *[Offstage]* Could you pass me the ... aaah ...

Bal2 *[Offstage]* Ooh! Careful where you put that ...

Bal3 [Offstage] Caught me right in the beg-your-pardon …

[Continue in quieter voice while MC talks over – of course I've not put on weight, it shrunk in the wash, that's all … well I don't know where you put it … etc]

MC Ahem, apologies for this, ladies and gentlemen. It seems that some of the cast have [Addressing door where Balthazar will enter] **FORGOTTEN TO TURN THEIR MIC OFF!**

Bal1,2,3 [Offstage] Oh, sorry. [Click]

MC Ummn, right, well, err. It seems there might be a short delay, so we could, ummn, we could … I know! How about a rousing chorus of Jingle Bells?

Choir Batman smells!

MC Noooo, no, no, no! Don't start that.
Alright, not Jingle Bells. We could do, err …

[**Balthazar** enters in a hurry, adjusting headdress]

Bal1 It's alright, it's alright.

Bal2 I'm here now, luvvies.

Bal3 Not too late, I hope?

MC [Loud whisper, trying to shoo him/them off] You're too early. You're not due on until after the choir.

Reading first, then the choir, then it's you.

Bal1	Oh, right you are. I'll just pop back here. *[Goes into corner, but comes straight back out]* You won't even know I'm here.
MC	Thanks.
Bal2	*[Popping back out]* I'll be quiet as a mouse.
MC	Great.
Bal3	*[Popping back out]* Not that I'm saying there are mice around, you understand.
MC	Yes, yes. Understood.
Bal1	*[Popping back out]* Ooh, just one tiny, weensy, little thing …
MC	*[Starting to get annoyed]* Yes?
Bal2	I've been listening to the choir …
MC	*[More annoyed]* Yes?
Bal3	and I heard what they sang last time …
MC	*[Penny drops]* Ah. Right.
Bal	and I think, *[Posh voice]* given my regal bearing and position of importance within the higher echelons of society,
Bal2	*[Posh voice]* plus the cultural significance of my elevated status,
Bal3	*[Common voice]* that they shouldn't go messing around and singing silly words about me.

MC Certainly, Mr Balthazar, sir. I'll make sure the choir behave themselves.
[Pointed look at choir, with 'I'm watching you' signs]

Choir *[Singing with exaggerated beauty]*

We three Kings of Orient are,
One in a taxi, one in a car,
One on a scooter, beeping his hooter,
Following yonder star.

Oh - star of wonder, star of light,
Sit on a box of dynamite,
Fly like a rocket, flames from your pocket,
You'll be a satellite.

*[**Choir** sniggers and looks guilty]*

Bal1 *[Marches to centre, arms folded and tapping foot]* What did I say? Hmm? What did I say?

MC *[Hanging head]* You said no silly words.

Bal2 No silly words. Exactly. And what did I get?

MC Silly words.
I'm sorry. I think Amos got at the choir again

*[**Amos** makes a rude face if onstage]*

Bal3 Amos, was it, eh? You just wait until this is over, Amos. I'll get my revenge. It'll be this *[Miming boxing]* and that for you. You just wait and see.

MC	Now, now Balthazar. It's Christmas. It's a time for peace, not for fighting.
Bal1	I'll give him peace, if I see that Amos. Peas and carrots all over his head. *[Boxing while being restrained by MC]*
Bal2	I'll make mincemeat of him. He's a right turkey. I'll give him a good stuffing.
Bal3	He's crackers if thinks he'll get away with this. I'll cream him to mash. I'll bash him in the mince pies. I'll … I'll
MC	*[Pulling Balthazar back]* Calm down, calm down. We don't want fisticuffs. This is a family show.
Bal1	But … but … *[Suddenly sagging]*
Bal2	Oh, I'm sorry. I'm so sorry. I don't really want to fight Amos. I'm rubbish at boxing anyway.
Bal3	It's just … *[Voice quavering]* … It's just …
MC	What is it, Balthazar?
Bal1	*[Bursting into tears]* It's the myrrh! *[Sobbing, like Myrr-rrr-rrr-rrh]*
MC	There, there. It's alright. Myrrh is a lovely gift.
Bal2	No it's not. It's a stupid gift. I should have brought nappies or baby clothes or a nice casserole. Even gold would have been useful, and frankincense is good for masking the smell. But

	noooooo. I had to get all posh and bring myrrh. What the heck use is that for a baby?
MC	Yes, I see.
Bal3	And then the camel ran out of fuel on the way here, and that made me late. And then I couldn't find my shoes and I missed my cue, and then when the choir sang that ... *[Sobbing]*
MC	... it was all just too much. Yes, I understand. Why don't you go and have a nice sit down, Balthazar? I'm sure the choir and Amos are *[Addressing choir]* **very sorry, aren't you**?

*[**Choir** and **Amos** look sorry]*

*[**Balthazar** exits if playing all characters, otherwise joins tableau]*

Suggested songs

From Heaven You Came (The Servant King)
In the Bleak Mid-winter
As with Gladness Men of Old

Scene 5 – Harold

Reading from John 1:1-14

> In the beginning was the Word.
> The Word was with God, and truly was God.
> From the very beginning, the Word was with God.
>
> Through this Word, God created all things.
> Nothing that was made, was made without him.
>
> Everything that was made received life from him, and his life gave light to everyone.
>
> This light is shining in the darkness,
> and darkness will never put it out.
>
> The Word became a human being,
> and made his home among us.
>
> We saw his true glory,
> the glory of the only Son of the Father,
> full of all God's kindness and truth.

[Adapt this section to invite children who are dressed as characters to join or form the tableau. Alternatively, have the speaking characters form the tableau, or show a picture on a screen.]

MC And now, as we near the end of our Nativity, I'd like to invite anyone to join our tableau. You could be Mary or Joseph, a shepherd, wise man or angel, or even one of the stable animals. *[Arrange children on stage]*

What a lovely picture this is of the first Christmas. I'm sorry that we had so many interruptions to the story.

*[**Harold** sidles on, MC tries to ignore him]*

I had hoped our Nativity would go a bit more smoothly than this, but things don't always happen the way we plan, do they?

Still, despite all the mess, we made it to the end. So all that remains is for me to wish everyone here the very best of Christmas blessings as we come to our final …

*[**Harold** sidles right up to MC]*

MC I'm sorry. Can I help you?

Harold I'm Harold. I'm an angel.

MC I can see that. *[Face falls]* Oh, hang on. You don't mean Harold as in 'Hark the **Harold** Angels sing', do you?

Harold *[Brightly]* Yes!

MC *[Emphatically]* No!
Just, no.
We don't need Harold angels.
It's just getting silly now.

[Losing it]

This was supposed to be a proper Nativity story, but everything's gone wrong.
Next thing you know it'll be 'most highly-flavoured gravy' and wise men on scooters beeping their hooters.

Choir We've already had that joke.

MC *[Shoulders sag]*
You know what? I give up. I give up trying to make this work.
It's been one thing after another going wrong and I give up.

> *[If you want a minister or head teacher to give the talk, they take over here, amending first line of the talk below to:*
>
> Never mind. You sit down for a moment. I know you wanted a nice, traditional Nativity and nothing went to plan.
>
> *Feel free to substitute your own talk in this section]*

I just wanted a nice, traditional Nativity and nothing went to plan.

Mind you, that was the same for the people in our story too.

Look at Mary. She didn't plan to have her baby in a borrowed shed. It was smelly and draughty and miles away from her home and family. It's not exactly what a young mum dreams of, is it?

And Joseph. What a massive guilt-trip. The whole journey was down to him, and he couldn't even find his wife a decent house to have a baby in. The carpenter who couldn't provide a bed for his son. He must have been chewed up inside.

The shepherds got in a mess, too. Maybe they weren't thinking straight because of the angels, but leaving the sheep alone wasn't a great idea. I wonder how many went missing while they were away, and I wonder how much trouble they got into.

And poor old Balthazar. I understand why he lost his temper. He was stressed up to the eyeballs and it all got too much for him.

They're not very different from us, really. How many of us plan a perfect Christmas only to find that, like Mary, things don't work out how we'd hoped? Or, like Joseph, we feel a failure because we can't do what we think is expected of us. Like the shepherds, we make bad decisions and then have to deal with the fall out. Like Balthazar, we have high expectations of the festivities and of ourselves, and the pressure all gets a bit much.

Real life isn't like the Christmas adverts. Real life is, if we're honest, a bit of a mess.

So this Christmas, I have some Good News. Good News for you. Good News for me. Good News, as the angels said, for the whole world.

God's OK with mess.

The reading we've just heard, from the start of John's Good News, says that God made his home with us. Right here in the mess and the stuff that didn't work out as planned.

God With Us. That's what the word Immanuel means – it's one of the names we give to Jesus. Jesus is God With Us. Right here. Right now.

God knows about the plans that didn't work out. God knows about the gnawing guilt. God knows about the bad decisions. God knows about the sadness behind the smile. And you know what? God still loves you.

And that's very Good News

[Turning to Harold / MC re-enters]

MC So, Harold? You come on right in. I'm sorry I snapped at you. It's not been the Nativity I hoped for, but that's not your fault.

*[**Harold** joins tableau]*

Let's go with Hark the Harold Angels and rejoice that God really is with us, even with our messy lives and lumpy gravy.

And a Merry, Messy Christmas to us all.

All *[Waving]*
Merry Christmas!

Suggested songs

Hark the Herald Angels Sing
It Came Upon the Midnight Clear
Light of the world (Here I am to Worship)
Shine, Jesus, Shine
O Come All Ye Faithful

Away in a Suitcase

A (Twenty) First Century Nativity

Away in a Suitcase

If Christmas happened today, what would it be like?

'Away in a Suitcase' is a funny, festive yet poignant retelling of the Nativity story set in modern times. Mary and Joseph's hotel room has been double-booked by three visiting foreigners. There are no travel cots left, so they use a suitcase as their baby's first bed.

Explore the Christmas story in today's world with a charming transformation to a traditional crib at the end. 'Away in a Suitcase' will leave you smiling, laughing and thinking.

The play has a running time of 20-25 minutes, longer if you add carols between the scenes, and includes a short Christmas message from the narrator or another speaker such as a head teacher or a minister.

There are parts suitable for a range of abilities, with a minimum cast of 19 adjustable to 30 or more. The costumes are deliberately simple, and there are few props and little scenery.

'Away in a Suitcase' is perfect for your Crib Service, All-Age Worship, Messy Church or school Nativity play.

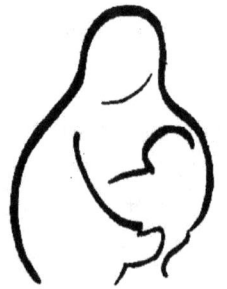

Cast

There are 11 main speaking parts, including a Narrator and all the traditional characters. These are best suited to more-confident actors.

For those who are less confident, there are choruses of Hotel Staff and Angels. These act and speak as groups, perfect for those who do not want a main part but want more than walk-ons. Finally, there are optional non-speaking parts for younger children.

Speaking Parts

- **Narr**   Narrator, 'reads' from large Bible
- **Mary**   College student
- **Mum**   Practical and friendly
- **Gabriel**   Cool. Think 'The Fonz'
- **Joe**   Likes computer games
- **Manager**   Ultra-polite and apologetic
- **Amos**   Boss shepherd
- **Laban**   Apprentice shepherd
- **Balthazar** Wise man
- **Melchior** Wise man
- **Caspar**   Wise man
- **Postie**   Same person as Mum

Chorus Parts

- **Hotel Staff**   5 to 10 tall people to form 'wall'
- **Angels**   4 to 12 people

Non-Speaking Parts

- **Sheep**   5 to 15 children (optional)

If you need a larger cast, form a choir to lead the carols between scenes. You can also have scene introducers who walk on stage with a large sign and announce each scene. They can join the transformation scene at the end by adding tinsel and surrounding the tableau.

A Note on Angels

When we think of angels in children's nativity plays, most of us imagine cute little girls in pigtails and tinsel.

Angels in the Bible, however, are powerfully masculine. Think of Arnold Schwarzenegger or Dwayne 'The Rock' Johnson. (That's why the first thing angels say is almost always 'Do not be afraid.')

So, while you may choose to cast Gabriel's chorus of angels as small, cute and glittery, Gabriel himself should be tall, confident and cool.

Costumes

Most characters are initially in modern dress and transform into traditional costumes ready for the final reveal. They do this behind a 'wall' made from Hotel Staff and Angels.

Costumes do not have to be complex. Modern dress can be jeans and a hoodie, or a white shirt or t-shirt with school uniform trousers.

You can make simple robes with a blanket draped like a cloak and the ever-present checked tea towel, or you can use supermarket nativity costumes.

If possible, avoid clothing that needs to go over the head because the change into traditional costumes happens on stage. Zip-up hoodies are great because they are easy to take off, and you can hide a whole lot underneath.

Many characters transform into angels for the final reveal. They wear white shirts or t-shirts as part of their modern dress, then remove any outer layer (jacket, apron, etc) and add a lollipop-shaped piece of tinsel. This can be worn as a halo with the tail down the back, or as a tie by placing the loop under a shirt collar. They can hide the tinsel halos/ties in a pocket until needed for the final reveal.

Costume suggestions (→ transformation)

Narr White shirt, black/grey trousers
→ Add tinsel halo/tie if joining the crib scene

Mary Blue dress tucked up under zip-up hoodie, leggings, cushion & baby
→ Remove hoodie, add blue shawl draped over head, swap cushion for baby

Mum/Postie White shirt, jeans and coloured cardigan
→ Remove cardigan, add cap and parcel to become Postie

Gabriel Leather jacket, white shirt or t-shirt, jeans, big boots, optional wings
→ Remove jacket, add tinsel halo/tie

Joe Robe tucked up under zip-up hoodie, jeans
→ Remove hoodie, add head dress

Manager White shirt, black/grey trousers and jacket
→ Remove jacket, add tinsel halo/tie

Staff White shirt, black/grey trousers, apron
→ Remove apron, add tinsel halo/tie

Shepherds Robe tucked up under zip-up hoodie, high-vis jacket, jeans
→ Remove hoodie and high-vis, add head dress

Sheep Sheep costume, or party clothes and holding sheep toy
(You can have one child dressed as a cow or donkey as a joke for the shepherds)
→ No change

Angels All in white with tinsel belt, or Christmas jumper, jeans, tinsel halo/tie
→ No change

Wise Men Robe tucked up under white lab coat
→ Remove lab coat, add optional crown or beard

Postie White shirt, jeans, cap, parcel
→ Remove cap, add tinsel halo/tie

Props

Large comfy armchair

Free-standing door (optional)

Scene 1	large Bible (Narr) also throughout textbook (Mary)
Scene 2	VR headset (Joe) phone (Joe)
Scene 3	cushion (Mary) letter (Joe) phone (Joe)
Scene 4	cushion (Mary) suitcase with clothes (Joe)
Scene 5	2 chairs, two mugs (Amos and Laban)
Scene 6	3 travel bags containing: Lynx Gold gift set (Bal) large bottle marked 'Frankincense' (Mel) large hand cream (Cas)
Scene 7	large parcel containing a phone (Postie) box or small stool (Gabriel) Jesus doll (Mary)

Staging

There is a large comfy chair centre stage, not too near the front. There needs to be enough room in front of the chair for the suitcase and two rows of children (which hide the assembling crib scene), and for scenes 5, 6 & 7 to happen in front of that.

Behind the chair is a box or small stool, and a doll wrapped in a pillowcase. The VR headset (safety goggles painted black) is at one side of the chair.

At one side of the stage, towards the front, there is a real or imaginary door to the outside. All characters entering and leaving to the outside go through this door. Other entrances and exits happen at the other side or as convenient.

Stage directions are given *in italics*. Stage directions at the end of a scene happen while the next scenes take place. For example, at the end of scene 4, Mary changes into traditional costume during scenes 5 and 6. You do not wait for her to do this before starting scene 5.

Two sound effects are needed: something falling over, and a knock at the door.

If it is possible, dim the lights at the back of the stage over the crib scene at the end of scene 4, then raise the lights for the final reveal, at the end of scene 7.

Crib Scene

During scenes 4, 5 and 6, a traditional crib scene builds up around the chair. The main characters are hidden behind a wall made of Hotel Staff, Angels and other characters. The wall opens to reveal the crib scene at the end of scene 7.

Assembling the Scene

Mary sits in the chair holding Jesus, and Joseph sits on the chair arm.

Manager places the open suitcase at Mary's feet for the manger.

The Shepherds stand to one side behind the chair, and the Wise Men to the other side, forming an arc.

Gabriel stands in the middle of the arc, directly behind the chair, on a box to give him height.

The Hotel Staff form the wall that hides the crib scene. The Angels form another wall in front of the Staff.

During the message, Hotel Staff transform to more Angels

The Reveal

The walls of Hotel Staff and Angels part to reveal the crib scene.

Angels and Hotel Staff stand or kneel to the left and right, framing the scene.

The sheep enter and sit on the floor at the front.

Mary places Jesus in the suitcase-manger by her feet.

Away in a Suitcase

The Script

Away in a Suitcase

Scene 1 – Mary's House

*[**Mary** enters slowly, reading a textbook, and flops sideways on a large comfy chair, centre stage]*

Narr   In the sixth month, God sent the angel Gabriel to Nazareth in Galilee.

[Knock at the door]

Mary   Muuuuuum! There's someone at the door.

Mum   *[Offstage]* Can you answer it, Mary?

Mary   I can't. I'm in the middle of college work.

Mum   And I'm in the middle of fixing your curtain rail, and if I'm not careful I'll ... ooo, errr, oh dear!

[Crash sound effect]

Mary   Oops.

Mum   I'm OK. I'm OK. Ooh, that's going to have a bruise in the morning.

[Knock at the door]

Mary   Daaaaaad! There's someone at the door.

Mum   Your dad's gone on a park run. You'll have to get it.

Mary   *[Getting up]* Oh, I s'pose.

[Knock at the door]

Alright, alright, I'm coming. Keep your wig on.

[*Mary* opens 'door', *Gabriel* steps inside]

Gabriel Greetings, you who are highly favoured! The Lord is with you.

Mary You what?

Gabriel Greetings, you who are highly favoured! The Lord is with you.

Mary [*Giving him a 'what planet are you on?' look*] R-i-i-i-ght. OK.

Gabriel Hello Mary, I am Gabriel. I have a message for you. From the boss. [*Pointing upwards*]

Mary Gabriel? You mean you're an ... How do you know my ...? A message from ...?
You'd better come in.

[*Both move to chair*]

Sit down?

Gabriel I think you might need the chair.

Mary Why?

Gabriel You're going to have a baby.

Mary [*Looking coy*] Well yes, probably, some day. But Joe and I only got engaged last month.
We've not even set a date for the wedding yet. We certainly weren't planning on having a baby anytime soon. I'm still at college!

Gabriel This will be God's son, not Joseph's.

Mary [*Sitting down suddenly*] But ... but ... I mean ... well ... y'know ... ummmmn ... how?

Gabriel Oh, *[Waving hands]* Holy Spirit and all that, you know.
You will give birth to a son, and you will name him Jesus. He will be great and will be called the Son of the Most High.

Mary Oh. Right. *[Talking to self, rapidly]* Wow! God's son? I mean, WOW! Why me? It's gobsmacking! It's incredible! How will I cope?
[Continue mumbling to self]

Gabriel *[Speaking over Mary]* So is that OK then?

Mary What? Oh, yes. Yes, let's do it!
[Talking to self again] Crumbs, God's baby! I wonder if he'll look like me?
What kind of nappies does God's son wear?
[Continue while Gabriel leaves]

Gabriel I'll let myself out, then. Bye.

*[**Gabriel** exits through 'door' and **Mum** enters from other side, wiping hands]*

Mum Who was that, dear?

*[**Mary** walks to Mum, taking textbook]*

Mary You'll never guess, Mum. You'll never guess!

*[**Mary** and **Mum** exit]*

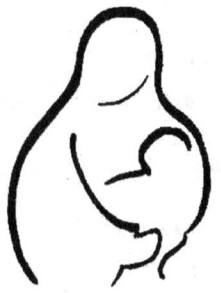

Scene 2 – Mary's House, a week later

Narr Now, Mary was pledged to be married to Joseph.

*[Knock at the door, **Mum** enters and answers door]*

Mum Hello, Joe dear. Come on in. You know Mary's away, staying with her cousin Elizabeth?

*[**Joe** enters, looking cross]*

Joe Yeah, I know she's away. That's why I've come round now. I got this text from her last night.

[Showing phone]
A baby? Did you know about this?

Mum Ah, yes dear. I know it looks bad but don't …

Joe *[Interrupting]* Looks bad? It feels bad! Right here. *[Thumps chest]*
She's broken my heart, that girl. Told me some rubbish about an angel visiting her.
Does she think I'm an idiot?

Mum No, Joe, not at all. She loves you. Come and sit down, dear.

Joe Loves me? Well, she's got a funny way of showing it! The wedding's off. *[Flops in chair]*
I've only come round to bring back her CDs.

Mum Now don't be hasty, dear.
Let me get you a cup of tea and you can have a go with that Minebox Playtendo game that you like so much.

*[**Mum** exits and changes character to **Postie**]*

Joe Yeah, OK then. Thanks.

[Puts on VR headset and starts miming]
What was I playing? Oh yes, Aerobatics Ace.

Resume.

Bank left ... bank right ... deploy ailerons ... barrel roll ... ah, this is great.

Ooh, thunder cloud ahead!

I'll power up and climb above it.
Raise elevators
[Mimes steep climb]

Wow! The view up here is brilliant.
[Looking round] Great graphics.

*[**Gabriel** enters and walks round Joe]*

Joe *[Watching Gabriel as he walks around]*
Amazing detail! That angel looks so real.
I could almost reach out and touch him.

Gabriel Joseph!

Joe Woo! Great 3D sound too!

Gabriel Joseph! Don't be afraid to take Mary as your wife, because her baby is from the Holy Spirit.

She will give birth to a son, and you will name him Jesus, because he will save his people from their sins.

[***Joe**'s jaw drops. **Gabriel** exits. Joe watches him in stunned silence]*

Joe   *[Removing headset]*
What just happened there?

[Addressing Mum, offstage]
Er, you know what I said about the wedding? Forget that. It's back on.

And could I have a couple of sugars in my tea, please?

[***Joe** exits, taking headset]*

Scene 3 – Mary's House, several months later

Narr In those days Caesar Augustus issued a decree that all people must register ...

[**Joe** and **Mary** enter, Joe is reading a letter, Mary is heavily pregnant]

Mary What's that you're reading, Joe?

Joe A letter from the Inland Revenue. We have to register Junior's name if we want a tax rebate for him.

Mary Already? He's not even born yet!
[Flops into chair]

Joe Yeah, it's a slow process. They've got a backlog as long as the orbit of Jupiter.

Mary So do we fill in a form, or can we do it online?

Joe Neither. We have to register in person. They have an open day next week at their office in Bethlehem. We could go to that.

Mary Do I have to go too?

Joe Yeah, sorry. They need both of us.
We could make it like a holiday, a mini-break in Bethlehem, call in and visit some of the relatives. You could go shopping or have a spa day with my cousin June. You two get on really well. What do you say?

Mary I dunno. The baby's nearly due and I feel like a whale on legs.

Joe I'll make it OK. I'll book us a nice hotel and we'll be back before Junior comes along.

Mary Oh, alright then.
Give us a hand up, will you?

[**Joe** and **Mary** struggle to get Mary our of chair]

But somewhere nice, mind. None of your manky Travel Inn Express.

Joe Whatever you say, my sweet.
[Tapping on phone]
Full English breakfast or continental?

[**Joe** and **Mary** exit, Joe still tapping on phone]

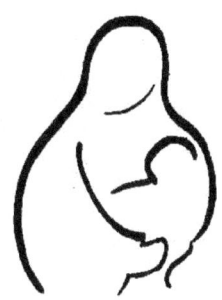

Scene 4 – Hotel Bethlehem

Narr So Joseph went to the town of Bethlehem with Mary, who was expecting a baby.

[**Mary** and **Joe** enter, Joe has a suitcase]

Joe I'm sorry, Mary, sweetheart. I know you didn't want Travel Inn Express, but everywhere else was booked up solid. And this was their last room.

Mary Joe, I'm so tired after that long journey that all I want is a nice comfy bed.

Joe You relax, dear. I'll get the keys.
[Puts suitcase down, mimes desk bell] PING!

[**Manager** enters, bowing obsequiously]

M'ger Good evening sir, madam, and welcome to the Hotel Bethlehem. How may I help you?

Joe Hello. I made a reservation online. Room 25-12. Could we have our keys, please?

M'ger Oh dear. Room 25-12?

Joe Yes. Is there a problem?

M'ger Indeed there is, sir. I do wish sir had rung to confirm. Room 25-12 is unavailable, I'm afraid.

Mary [Very quiet] Joe.

Joe What! I booked it last week!

M'ger If sir had read the small print, he would have noted that online reservations expire at 10pm.

	It is now 10:05, sir. And rooms are in great demand.
Mary	[Quiet] Joe.
Joe	So you've given our room to someone else?
M'ger	Indeed. Although sir will be pleased to know that his small oversight has provided accommodation to three foreign VIPs, here for an astronomy conference, I gather. They were very happy to find a vacant room in the middle of Bethlehem. Sir is so kind.
Mary	[Medium loud] Joe.
Joe	But where are we going to stay? Do you have any other rooms?
M'ger	I'm afraid not, sir. We are like a brand-new library – fully booked. [Silly laugh]
Mary	[Getting louder] Joe.
Joe	I suppose you don't have … ummmn … like … a stable round the back, or anything, do you?
M'ger	A Stable? Sir is having a laugh. Where do you think this is, Old MacDonald's Farm?
Mary	[Loud, tugging Joe's sleeve] Joe!
Joe	[Finally noticing] What is it, Mary?
Mary	The baby! It's coming!
Joe	[Horrified] What, now?
Mary	Now!

M'ger   Now? Oh, my word! A baby?
[To wings] Staff! Staff!
[To Joe] You can use my office. There's a snack machine and free Wi-Fi.

[Hotel **Staff** hurry on]

[To Hotel Staff]
Take these good people to my office and make them as comfortable as possible.
Break out the emergency pot noodles if you need to.

Staff   [Speaking all together or different lines for different people]
The emergency pot noodles?
Certainly sir!
[To Mary and Joe]
Come this way, please.

[**Mary**, **Joe** and **Staff** move to chair.
Mary sits on chair and **Joe** kneels beside (he will sit on the arm for the big reveal).

Staff form a wall in front of chair, backs to the audience, hiding Mary and Joe.

Manager paces around stage.]

M'ger   Oh dear, oh dear, oh dear! There was nothing about this in the staff training manual.

They'll need baby clothes.
Ummmn ... Oh! A pillowcase will do nicely.
Now what about a bed? All the travel cots are in use.

[Spots Joe's suitcase]
Perfect!
[To Mary and Joe]
Look! You can use this suitcase as a cot for the baby!

*[**Manager** takes suitcase behind the wall and places it open at Mary's feet.*

Manager *joins wall.*

While hidden, **Mary** *and* **Joe** *change to traditional clothes.*
Mary *hides her cushion behind the chair and gets Jesus doll.*

If possible, dim the lights over the crib scene until the reveal at the end of Scene 7.]

Scene 5 – Hillside Hut

Narr And there were shepherds abiding in the fields, keeping watch over their flocks by night.

*[**Amos** and **Laban** enter, each with a chair and mug, and place chairs centre stage, in front of wall of Staff]*

Amos *[Sitting]* Ah, modern technology. It's great, innit?

Laban *[Sitting]* Yeah.

Amos I mean, when I was training to be a shepherd, we didn't have none of this tech.
[Indicating imaginary screens in front of them]
None of these closed-circuit TVs and drones and whatnot.
Oh no. We had to watch sheep by actually watching them. Out in the cold, all seated on the ground.

Laban Yeah.

Amos It's so much better these days, sat in our cosy cabin, with a fully-automatic sock washer and endless cups of tea, eh?

Laban Yeah.

*[**Amos** and **Laban** clink mugs]*

Amos Anyway *[Looking at watch]* it's time to count the sheep.

Laban Yeah.

[As Amos names each sheep, a child runs on stage and waves (if dressed as a sheep) or holds up sheep toy, then runs off.

If you do not have children playing sheep, Laban spots each sheep in the audience as Amos names them.

Adjust the number of sheep to suit. Amos can use a list if needed.

If you have one child dressed as a cow/donkey, Amos and Laban are silent and then shrug as the child runs on stage, waves, and runs off.]

Amos Right, there's
[*First sheep runs on stage*]
Baatholemew,
Lambert,
Fleeceity,
Bert**ram**,
Ewenice,
Rambo,
Baarbara,
Pet**ewe**nia,
Rameses,
Baatimeaus,
J**ewe**dy,
Ramona,
Al**baa**rt and
Shaun.

Yep, that's the lot.

Time for more tea. Put the kettle on, Laban.
[***Amos** hands **Laban** his mug*]

Laban Why do I always make the tea, Amos? It must be your turn.

Amos *[Pointing to self]* Who's got BTec Certified Shepherding Level Two?
[Pointing to Laban] Who's the apprentice? Make the tea!

[Knock at the door]

Who's that? It's the middle of the night and we're miles from nowhere out here!

*[**Laban** opens the 'door' and stands staring outside with mouth open]*

Amos Tell 'em to come in quick, they're letting all the heat out. And make sure they wipe their feet. I'm not having muddy wellies all over my nice clean cabin.

Laban I … I … I don't think they're wearing wellies, Amos. *[Stands back to let Gabriel in]*

*[**Gabriel** strides in]*

Gabriel *[Loud voice]* Do not be afraid!

Am/Lab ARGHHHHHH! *[Both run screaming to other side of stage]*

Gabriel *[To audience]* This always happens.
[To shepherds] Seriously. I'm not going to bite you. Did I hear the kettle?

*[**Amos** opens and closes his mouth like a goldfish, pointing at Gabriel]*

Laban   Er, yes. I was just making tea. Would you like some?

Gabriel   Oh yes. I'm parched. *[Sitting]*

Amos   *[Still looking like a goldfish]* Whaa ... whaa ... whaa ...

Gabriel   *[To Laban, nodding at Amos]* Is he alright?

Laban   He wants to know what you are doing here. We don't get angels knocking on our door every night.

Gabriel   Oh yes. Sorry. Nearly forgot.

[Standing and proclaiming]
Behold, I bring you good news of great joy.
Your Saviour is born today in Bethlehem.
He is Christ, the Lord.

And this is how you will know him: You will find the baby wrapped in a pillowcase and lying in a suitcase.

[Looking puzzled and addressing someone offstage]
Are you sure that's the right line? 'Cos I thought it was ... No, it **is** right? ... You sure? ... OK.

[Proclaiming again]
...and lying in a suitcase!

[Sitting and addressing the door]
Come on in, team!

[**Angels** enter and stand along front of stage

if using two groups of angels, number them alternately 1 & 2 across the stage.
All of group 1 speak together, then all of group 2.
Alternatively, all angels speak both lines.]

Narr [*While angels get into place*]
And suddenly, with the angel there was a multitude of the heavenly host, praising God and saying:

Angels 1 [*Raising arms*] Glory to God in the highest heaven!

Angels 2 [*Raising arms*] Peace on earth, and good will to all people!

Laban [*Pause*] Crikey!

Amos [*Pause*] Yeah.

Laban C'mon, let's go and find this baby. What did he say, in a suitcase? Weird!

[**Gabriel** *exits, taking the chairs with him.*

Amos *and* **Laban** *move behind the wall and form half of arc to one side of the chair, kneeling to remain hidden. They change into traditional dress.*

Angels *form a second row of wall, in front of Hotel Staff, backs towards audience]*

Scene 6 – Hotel Bethlehem

Narr   And wise men came from the east saying …

[Balthazar, Melchior and Caspar enter]

Bal   … 'where is the one born king of the Jews?' is the question I would be asking if I didn't have a much bigger question on my mind.

Mel   What question is that, Balthazar?

Cas   Is it 'Why have we only got one hotel room for three of us?'

Bal   Er, no, but that is a good question. Who booked the room?

Bal/Cas   *[Pointing]* MELCHIOR!

Mel   It was all I could get! The other hotels were booked up solid. I only got this room because some other guests didn't turn up.

Cas   Oh well, it'll do I suppose. But if it's not the room, what is Balthazar's question?

Bal   I'm glad you asked, Caspar. *[Striking 'thoughtful' pose]* It is a question that wise men like us have wrestled with since the dawn of time.

[Bal gazes into the middle-distance. Mel and Cas follow his gaze, wondering what he's looking at]

>   A question of eternal significance and timeless consequence.
>   A question that rivals DNA in complexity, and

	exceeds the ability of the human brain to fathom.
Mel/Cas	What is the unending question, O wise and knowledgeable one?
Bal	Where on earth is our luggage?
Mel	Our luggage?
Cas	Are you saying that the airline lost our bags? Again?
Bal	Yes! It's a complete disaster, a total nightmare, a catastrophe, a tragedy, a cataclysm, a ...
Mel	[Interrupting] Calm down, Balthazar! Losing our luggage is not that bad.
Cas	Yes. We can always buy more socks tomorrow.
Bal	It's not the socks, boys. Haven't you realised?

[**Mel** and **Cas** look blank]

    The gifts?

[**Mel** and **Cas** look blank]

    For the new baby king?

[**Mel** and **Cas** look blank]

All	[Realising] They're in the suitcases!
Bal	What are we going to do? We can't turn up empty-handed. He'll think we're a right bunch of cheapskates.
Mel	Maybe we've got something in our hand luggage.

Cas For a baby? I don't think I packed a teddy bear in my carry-on.

Bal The original gifts weren't exactly child-friendly. These can't be any worse.
[Rummaging]
I've got this shower gel and shaving foam set.
[Shows Lynx Gold]

[**Mel** and **Cas** give him a questioning look, miming shaving]

Bal He'll ... grow into it?

Mel [Rummaging]
I got this for my mum from the duty free.
[Shows large perfume bottle, mimics advert with heavy French accent]
Frankincense, eau de parfam, pour homme, pour femme, pour vous.

[**Bal** and **Cas** look at each other and shrug]

Cas Yeah, right.
[Rummaging] Here's something a bit more practical.
[Shows bottle of hand cream]
Moisturising hand cream [Reading label] with aloe vera and myrrh. Perfect for the royal botty. Don't want him getting nappy rash now, do we?

Bal Good, that's all settled. Now, it's getting late. We should try to find the baby.
I'll ring down to the front desk and ask the manager if he knows anything.
[Mimes using phone]

Hello? Yes, it's the three gents in room 25-12. Would you happen to know anything about a new baby?
[Listens] ... Yes, that's right. A new baby. Born this night. In Bethlehem.
[Listens] ... You do? [To others] He does!

[**Mel** and **Car** cheer]

He's in this hotel? [To others] He's in this hotel!

[**Mel** and **Car** cheer]

Mmhhm, mmhhm. OK, thanks. Bye.
[Puts 'phone' down]

Mel   Well?

Cas   Where is he?

Bal   He's in the manager's office. It's just off the lobby, downstairs. You remember when we came in, there was that large, spiky lampshade? The manager's office is right underneath that.

Mel   So you mean we ...

Cas   ... just have to ...

All   ... follow the star!

[**Bal**, **Mel** and **Cas** move behind the wall and form other half of arc to the side of the chair, kneeling to remain hidden. They change into traditional costume.]

Scene 7 – Right Here, Right Now

*[During the message, Hotel **Staff** remove aprons and add tinsel halos/ties to become more **Angels**.*

All other characters remove jackets, hoodies etc and get ready for the big reveal.

*The message can be delivered by
the **Narrator** (use first section),
or by a different **Speaker** (use second section)*

*Keep lights dim over crib scene if possible, or have **Narrator/Speaker** move away to one side so that people don't notice cast changing]*

If Narrator is giving message

Narr   And it came to pass that there was delivered upon that night the greatest gift of all time.

*[**Postie** enters with large parcel]*

Postie   Delivery!

Narr   *[Taking parcel]* Thanks.

Postie   Sign here.

*[**Postie** offers hand, **Narr** signs hand]*

Postie   Careful, it's fragile.

*[**Postie** joins Hotel Staff in wall and changes costume]*

Narr   Oh, I'll be careful …

If Speaker is giving message

Narr And it came to pass that there was delivered upon that night the greatest gift of all time.

[**Postie** enters with large parcel]

Postie Delivery for [Name of speaker]!

Speaker [Taking parcel] Thanks.

Postie Sign here.

[**Postie** offers hand, **Speaker** signs hand]

Postie Careful, it's fragile.

[**Postie** and **Narr** join Hotel Staff in wall and change costume]

Speaker Oh, I'll be careful …

Christmas Message

Oh, I'll be careful, don't you worry. I've been waiting for this for such a long time.

[Carefully opening box]
This is the one that we all have been expecting. The promised one. The one spoken of from ages past. The one who changes everything. The greatest gift of all time.

[Gently takes out and cradles new phone]
Isn't he lovely?
[Talking to phone like a baby]
Yes, you are. You're so lovely. Who's the best phone in the world? You are!

[Noticing audience]
What? Isn't this the great gift of all time?

Maybe you're right. I mean, Christmas presents are great (Ta very much for the phone, Mum) but in a few months they'll bring out a new model and this one won't be so trendy any more.

And the food at Christmas is great, all the roast potatoes and fancy nibbles, but come the day after Boxing Day we're all sick of it.

And the glitz and glitter of Christmas, I love it! I love the decorated trees and the lights and the Christmas films on the telly, but it won't be long before we clear it away and go back to real life.

There's lots about Christmas that is great, but it doesn't last. When the holiday ends and we're back at work, back at school, will it have made any difference? Is a few days of over-eating and wearing novelty jumpers all there is?

This play has told us about the most famous birthday on earth, and we watch it once a year then pack it away in a box marked 'Cute Stuff for Kids', or 'Ancient Myths and Legends'.

Is that all it is? Sure, it happened a long time ago, but this isn't a fairy tale. Even the Roman historians agree that Jesus was a real person.

So what if …

What if this isn't just a cute story for kids? Does it make a difference that this baby grew up and told me to love my enemies and forgive people who don't deserve it? That's really hard. I can't say that I manage it.

But what if ...

What if God is not Santa, and life is not about being on the naughty list or nice list?

The Bible says that none of us are good enough to be on the nice list, and God knows that, so there's no point pretending.

But God doesn't leave us on the naughty list; he does something to fix it. God sent Jesus to move us to the nice list because Jesus **is** good enough.

So what if ...

What if this first-century story still happens today, in the twenty-first-century? I wonder who I would be in the scene: a not-so-wise man perhaps, or the hotel waiter who brought the pot noodle. I wonder who you would be.

This Christmas, I wonder where we will meet Jesus, God with us, born as the child who changes everything.

[Turns to watch as crib scene is revealed]

Revealing the Transformation

If lights have been dimmed, raise them now.

Gabriel *walks to centre stage with jacket over shoulder.*

Gabriel *gives his jacket to* ***Narr/Speaker*** *and adds tinsel halo/tie in view of audience.*

Gabriel *walks behind wall and stands on box behind chair. He should be clearly visible.*

Gabriel *lifts his arms*

(The next items all happen at once)

> *Play intro to 'Silent Night'*
>
> ***Gabriel*** *slowly opens arms wide.*
>
> ***Wise Men*** *and* ***Shepherds*** *stand.* ***Joe*** *sits on arm of chair.*
>
> *As Gabriel opens his arms,* ***Angels*** *(inc* ***Staff***, ***Manager*** *etc) part and move to sides to reveal the crib scene.*

Angels *turn faces toward crib scene and hold out arms across body towards suitcase.*

Sheep *enter and sit around suitcase.*

All *watch as* ***Mary*** *places Jesus in the suitcase at her feet.*

All *sing first verse of 'Silent Night'.*

About the Author

Hi, I'm Fay.

In no particular order, I am a mum, choc-o-holic, mathematician, author, blogger, knitter, children's worker and mad scientist.

I write The Reflectionary, a weekly blog of original resources for churches, youth groups, children's work and schools' ministry.

Everything is free, so pop along and help yourself at www.reflectionary.org. You can sign up there to have the posts sent straight to your mailbox. No spam ever, I promise!

I studied Theology at Spurgeon's College and at Wesley House, Cambridge, specialising in children's spirituality, and I'm a trainee Lay Minister in the Church of England. You can find links to my published academic works at www.fayrowland.co.uk.

When not writing or studying, I teach maths for a living and spend most of the rest of the time being creative. I worship at a large Anglican church in the English Midlands, where I'm part of the teams for all-age worship and Messy Church.

I live with my children and pet dragon in an untidy house full of noise and glue sticks and mess (which I blame on the kids, but really, it's me).

Other Publications

A Bucketful of Ideas for Church Drama (the green one)

"Parables as Jesus would have told them – witty and thought-provoking."

#1 Best-Seller in Puppet Scripts!

"Thirty Pieces of Chocolate is a fine pun-run."

A(nother) Bucketful of Ideas for Church Drama (the blue one)

14 scripts including CRISP-tingle, a pop-up nativity, and lots more.

"Delivers the timeless truths of scripture in a modern and punchy manner."

So You've finished Writing. Now What?

Best-selling non-fiction author, Fay guides you with humour and helpful insight through the maze of the editing process and out into the wonderful world of publishing.

So what are you waiting for, the credits?

Walking to Bethlehem

25 imaginative devotions for adults and children, with reflective colouring and craft ideas.

"Travel from BC to AD to focus your mind on the road to Bethlehem. Fun and devotional, practical and creative."

#1 Best-Seller in Advent Devotions!

The Big Story

Discover the Bible as one big story of God and God's people, from the very beginning of everything up to the wonder of Easter.

Perfect for personal devotions, for weekly Bible studies and youth groups, discover The Big Story today.

Broken Bits & Weirdness

Meet nine of the Bible's dismal failures and learn how God still loves them (and us), even with our Broken Bits & Weirdness.

With Bible notes, crafts, cooking, colouring and other resources, and studies for Good Friday and Easter Day, this is perfect for Lent or any time of year.

#1 Best-Seller in Bible Meditations!

Creativity Matters

Join thirteen authors as they share their passion for why you should write in their genre and find your own passion as you read.

In my chapter, 'Why Write Drama?', you can discover what makes drama sparkle, and why you shouldn't take your gran to see a Greek satyr play!

URC Prayer Handbooks

I have been a commissioned author for the URC's prayer handbooks for several years.

They are full of original, passionate, quirky and relevant prayers, with each Sunday having several prayers linked to readings from the Revised Common Lectionary. They are suitable for both congregational and private use, using contemporary language and covering a broad range of topics.

Available from the URC's website shop.

www.ingramcontent.com/pod-product-compliance
Lightning Source LLC
Chambersburg PA
CBHW050251120526
44590CB00016B/2312